George Washington Carver

An Innovative Life

written by Elizabeth MacLeod

Kids Can Press

With best wishes and thanks to Patricia for all of her inspired work on the books in this series.

Acknowledgments

Many thanks to Diane Eilenstein, Curtis Gregory, Lana Henry and Dena Matteson at the George Washington Carver National Monument.

Very special thanks to editor Chris McClymont for sowing the seeds, tilling the soil and making this book grow. Thank you for all of your help, Chris. The fabulous look of yet another book in this series is due to the talent, skill and perseverance of Karen Powers, designer. I so appreciate her hard work.

Many thanks to everyone at Kids Can Press, especially production editor Daniel Naccarato.

I am so sorry that this is the last book in this series on which Patricia Buckley will perform photo researching duties. Her creativity, organization and sense of humor will be greatly missed by the whole Snapshots team.

Thanks as ever to Dad, John and Douglas. And special thanks and love to Paul, my favorite co-worker out in the field.

Kids Can Press acknowledges the financial support of the Government of Ontario, through the Ontario Media Development Corporation's Ontario Book Initiative; the Ontario Arts Council; the Canada Council for the Arts; and the Government of Canada, through the BPIDP, for our publishing activity.

Published in Canada by
Kids Can Press Ltd.
29 Birch Avenue
Toronto, ON M4V 1E2

Published in the U.S. by
Kids Can Press Ltd.
2250 Military Road
Tonawanda, NY 14150

www.kidscanpress.com

Series editor: Valerie Wyatt
Edited by Christine McClymont
Designed by Karen Powers
Printed and bound in Singapore

The hardcover edition of this book is smyth sewn casebound.
The paperback edition of this book is limp sewn with a drawn-on cover.

CM 07 0 9 8 7 6 5 4 3 2 1
CM PA 07 0 9 8 7 6 5 4 3 2 1

Library and Archives Canada Cataloguing in Publication

MacLeod, Elizabeth
    George Washington Carver : an innovative life / written by Elizabeth MacLeod.

(Snapshots: images of people and places in history)
Includes index.

ISBN-13: 978-1-55337-906-5 (bound)   ISBN-10: 1-55337-906-3 (bound)
ISBN-13: 978-1-55337-907-2 (pbk.)   ISBN-10: 1-55337-907-1 (pbk.)

1. Carver, George Washington, 1864?–1943 — Juvenile literature.
2. African American agriculturists — Biography — Juvenile literature.
3. Agriculturists — United States — Juvenile literature. I. Title.

S417.C3M33 2007   j630.92   C2006-903391-9

Kids Can Press is a *corus*™ Entertainment company

Contents

Meet George Washington Carver

I created pickles, shampoo and more from peanuts. I also came up with more than 160 products using sweet potatoes.

It's hard to believe that something as small as a peanut can change a person's life. But peanuts certainly altered the career of George Washington Carver. He went from being a little-known professor to a world-famous peanut scientist. George created more than 325 products from peanuts, including substitutes for rubber, meat and wood stains.

But George's most important work was improving agriculture in the southern United States. He introduced people to the idea of crop rotation to improve the soil and control insects and diseases (find out more on page 20). George also taught farmers to enrich their soil by planting crops such as peanuts and soybeans. George's ideas turned the southern economy around.

Much more than a scientist and a farming expert, George was also an inspiring teacher, gifted painter and talented musician. Though born the son of a slave, he became a symbol of African American success and interracial harmony.

During his lifetime, George was admired by many famous people, including inventor Thomas Edison, carmaker Henry Ford and U.S. President Franklin Delano Roosevelt. He continues to inspire people today.

When George became a professor at Tuskegee Institute (now Tuskegee University), he joined a group of people dedicated to educating Black students and helping them realize their full potential. Throughout his life, George quietly fought against racial prejudice.

How did George learn so much about plants and farming? What inspired him to teach and become an inventor? What was he really like?

H. W. Carver,

George used the middle name "Washington." Read the whole story on page 10.

George was a great professor and his students loved him. But he liked researching and working in his laboratory best.

The peanut plant is very unusual. After it flowers, its stalks send "pegs" into the ground so that the seed pods grow underground.

Many farmers couldn't make it to George's lectures, so he sent out farming experts to visit them in this truck.

Every day, George picked a fresh flower for his lapel.

George worked hard to teach Black farmers how to make their lives better by improving the way they farmed.

Country at war!

"Whenever I hear anyone arguing for slavery I feel a strong impulse to see it tried on him personally."

— Abraham Lincoln

Abraham Lincoln was the sixteenth president of the United States. He led the country from 1861 to 1865, when he was shot and killed by a man trying to help the Confederate side.

George Washington Carver never knew exactly when he was born, but he said it was "near the end of the war." The war he meant was the American Civil War, which took place between 1861 and 1865. The Union States, which were mostly northern states, battled the southern states, also known as the Confederate States of America.

There were many reasons why war broke out. Some Southerners complained that the southern states were taxed more heavily than the northern ones. Others felt that the powers the federal government held over the states weren't fair. But one of the big differences between the North and South was their attitude toward slavery.

Both George's mother and father were slaves. For more than 200 years, White people, especially those in the southern states, used Black slaves to work their farms or do chores. Enslaved people were not paid. They belonged to their owners and had no freedom or control over their lives.

Some White people were kind and cared for their slaves almost like family. But many were cruel — slaves died from beatings, disease or exhaustion. Families were broken up when the children of slaves were sold away.

Many enslaved people tried to escape from the cruel treatment. They longed to be free to live their own lives. Some journeyed to northern states where slavery was against the law. Southern slave owners were unhappy when Northerners helped runaway slaves.

When Abraham Lincoln, a Northerner, was elected president of the United States, everyone knew he was against slavery. Many White Southerners didn't think the new president would treat them fairly. Lincoln promised to keep slavery out of two new territories, Kansas and Missouri (where George would be born), and that was the last straw.

The southern states declared themselves separate from the United States. They formed the Confederate States of America with Jefferson Davis as their president, and the Civil War began. More than 600 000 Americans died during this long, destructive war. It finally ended with victory for President Lincoln and the Union states.

The win by the northern states resulted in the end of slavery in the United States. Although life didn't improve immediately for Black slaves, and they still faced racial prejudice, they were finally free.

About 180 000 Black soldiers fought for the Union States.

The Confederate battle flag featured 13 stars, one for each state in the Confederacy.

Jefferson Davis was the first and only president of the Confederate States of America.

" MAKE WAY FOR LIBERTY!"

Owners of the large farms, or plantations, in the South depended on unpaid slave labor to plant and harvest cotton, tobacco and other crops.

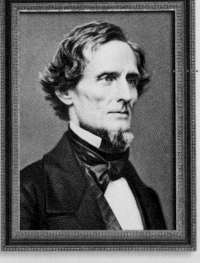

The stars on the Union flag represent the 35 states in the Union at the end of the Civil War. The bars stand for the country's original 13 states.

Most escaping slaves headed north to free states or to Canada. With no compasses to guide them, they followed the North Star.

Many Black slaves escaped with help from a network of White people and Black people known as the Underground Railroad.

Young George

"I literally lived in the woods. I wanted to know every strange stone, flower, insect, bird or beast."

— George

Sometimes George brought frogs or insects into the Carver house. Aunt Sue made him take them back outside just as soon as she discovered them!

George was born in about 1864 on a farm in Diamond Grove, Missouri. The farm's owner was Moses Carver. Moses had bought George's mother, Mary, in about 1855 because he couldn't find enough non-slave workers to help with the many chores on the farm. Mary helped with the housework and Moses and his wife, Susan, treated Mary more like family than an enslaved person.

Mary had a son, Jim, who was about five years older than George. George never knew his father. He was a slave on a nearby farm and was killed in a logging accident. Now no one even knows his name.

One night when George was very young, slave raiders kidnapped George and his mother. Moses hired a neighbor to bring them back. But the rescuer returned with George only — Mary was never seen again. George and Jim were now slave orphans.

Moses and Susan raised the boys as if they were their sons. George and Jim called the couple Uncle Mose and Aunt Sue, and took Carver as their own last name. Jim was strong and worked in the fields. But George was a small boy and often sick, so he helped Aunt Sue with indoor work such as laundry, cleaning and cooking.

When George's chores were done for the day, he headed off to collect rocks, insects and plants. He carefully dug up flowers and replanted them in a secret garden he kept. There he watched over them, finding out how to make them grow better.

George also helped Aunt Sue with her vegetable and flower gardens. He gained a reputation for being able to make any plant grow and was nicknamed "Plant Doctor." Years later, George's love of plants would make him famous around the world.

One day, when George was about 10, he helped a neighbor with her plants, then wandered into her house. He asked about the wonderful things on her walls. George had never before seen paintings and was fascinated by them. He began using berries and roots to make paints, and painted on boards, rocks, the ground and old cans. George enjoyed painting for the rest of his life.

IOWA

MISSOURI

KANSAS

ALABAMA

I was born in Missouri in Diamond Grove — it's now called Diamond. Later I lived in Kansas, Iowa and Alabama.

Diamond Grove

Moses Carver taught George to love music, be thrifty and have the courage to be different from other people.

George watched Aunt Sue knit, crochet and do needlepoint, and taught himself these crafts. Here is a needlepoint sampler he made.

George was weak when he was a boy and small for his age. He had a high-pitched voice, perhaps due to whooping cough and pneumonia.

George had an instinct for what plants need to thrive. He also learned how to observe them carefully.

The house where George was born is no longer standing. But you can see this replica of it at Greenfield Village in Dearborn, Michigan.

Thirst for education

"My soul thirsted for an education."

— George

On the Carver farm, George learned his alphabet, and this made him want to study more. But the nearest school was for White children only, so the Carvers hired a tutor for George. Soon he was asking questions that the tutor couldn't answer.

When George was about 12 years old, Moses and Susan decided he was old enough to move to the nearby town of Neosho, which had a school for African American children. There George stayed with Mariah and Andrew Watkins, who encouraged him to attend both school and church. With Aunt Mariah's help, George became an expert at cleaning laundry.

By the time George was 13 or so, he felt he'd learned everything he could at the school in Neosho. He moved to Fort Scott, Kansas, and stayed with another family. But George was never able to earn much money there. That meant he could only afford to attend school for a week or so at a time, then he'd have to drop out.

Even worse, on March 26, 1879, George saw a crowd drag an African American prisoner out of jail and hang him. The hatred and racial prejudice George saw shocked him, and he ran away from Fort Scott. Over the next few years, he held many jobs. He was happiest when he could work with plants. Whenever possible, George went to school and moved up from grade to grade.

As George traveled, he made many friends and enjoyed writing letters to them. But while staying in Minneapolis, Kansas, George found he was receiving very few letters back. Then he discovered there was another George Carver in town, and mail was going to the wrong address. George decided to add a middle initial to make his name unique — he chose "W." One of George's friends asked if the "W" stood for "Washington." "Why not?" George replied.

George lived in Minneapolis for four years. By now, he was about 20 years old and 1.8 m (6 ft.) tall, running a successful laundry business and attending school. He moved to Kansas City, then decided to apply to Highland College, in Highland, Kansas. George was very proud when he was accepted.

But when George showed up at Highland College, he was turned down — because of his color. He never forgot this rejection.

While still in Diamond Grove, at about age 10, George began attending church. Religion was important to George throughout his life.

After leaving Neosho, George moved around Kansas. He lived in Fort Scott, Olathe, Paola, Minneapolis, Kansas City and Highland.

"Aunt Mariah" Watkins was a nurse and taught George how to make medicines from plants.

George's school in Neosho was just as crowded as this one. Seventy-five students were crammed into a classroom smaller than most living rooms.

George (left) saw his brother Jim for the last time in 1883 during a visit to Missouri. Shortly after George returned to Kansas, he got word that Jim had died of smallpox.

Doing laundry helped me earn my way through school.

Homesteading

"Without genuine love of humanity, it is impossible to accomplish much in this question of the races."

— George

George enjoyed life on the prairies, despite fierce winter storms and burning summer droughts.

George worked in Highland, Kansas, for about a year to earn some money. Then in August 1886, when he was about 21, he headed to western Kansas to try something new: homesteading. The American government wanted to encourage people to move west. So it made land available at low cost to people willing to turn prairie into farmland.

Homesteading was difficult, and many people who tried it had to give up. It may have appealed to George because it's what Moses Carver had done in his younger days. It was also a chance for George to make a new start after being rejected at Highland College.

George settled on land near Beeler in Ness County, Kansas. He found his White neighbors to be mostly friendly, but he did run into racial prejudice. George sometimes told a story about working for nearby farmer George Steeley. Mr. Steeley's mother refused to let the African American newcomer eat with her and her son. Later, however, Mrs. Steeley left her son's farm, and the two Georges became good friends.

Western Kansas was like a desert. With no lumber or bricks for building homes, settlers had to be very creative. They built their houses out of thick pieces of sod cut from the land. George worked on the Steeley farm during the day, then his boss helped him build his house in the evenings. George's tiny sod house, or soddy, had just enough room for his bed, a table, chairs and a stove.

Once George had built his house, he could plant his own crops — corn and other vegetables. He hoped to be able to dig a well on his property, but couldn't find any water. That meant he had to haul water from the Steeley farm. Soon George had 42 ha (17 acres) of crops planted, and keeping them watered in the prairie heat was a tough job.

George enjoyed being close to nature, and he was recognized as one of the most educated people in the area. Some of the people he met here remained his friends for the rest of his life. But it wasn't long before George missed being in school. So after about three years of homesteading, he left Ness County. He had no clear idea what he would do next.

G.W. Carver.

Ever since George's days back in Diamond Grove, he had been interested in painting. In Ness County, he finally took his first art lesson. George used this paint palette for many years.

Because George could play accordion, he was very popular at community dances.

George loved drawing desert plants such as this cactus. When he left his homestead, he carried several cacti with him.

George learned to build sod houses like this one.

Western Kansas fascinated me because the land was so vast and empty.

College at last

"Miss Budd helped me in whatever way she could; often going far out of her way to encourage and see that I had such things as I needed."

— George

This is one of the oil paintings I created while at Simpson College. You can see it now at Tuskegee University.

From Kansas, George headed east and settled in Winterset, Iowa. The chef at one of the town's hotels was away for a few months, so George took over his job. George also became the food buyer. Because he knew how to be thrifty, he cut the hotel's food expenses in half!

George began attending a local church where his beautiful singing voice caught the attention of John and Helen Milholland. They became good friends — Helen helped George with his singing in return for art lessons.

When the chef returned to the hotel, George left and opened a laundry. But the Milhollands suggested he go back to school. They knew that Simpson College in nearby Indianola had already accepted an African American student.

The last time George had applied to a college, he'd been coldly rejected. But the Milhollands kept pushing him, and George remembered how much he enjoyed learning.

On September 9, 1890, George became Simpson College's second-ever African American student. The other students were around 16 or 17 years old, while George was about 26. He decided to study art. His teacher, Etta Budd, was soon impressed with his painting.

Paying the school fees was a struggle for George. He opened a laundry and lived in a tiny old shack, but he still had little money for food. However, Etta and her friend Sophia Liston found him a better place to live, as well as more customers for his laundry. When the other students discovered how little furniture George had, they bought him chairs and a table. They delivered the furniture when they knew George was out so he wouldn't be embarrassed.

Etta could see George was talented, but thought he might have a difficult time making a living as an artist, especially because African Americans faced racial prejudice. She could tell from his paintings that he was interested in plants. So Etta suggested George transfer to nearby Iowa State College (now Iowa State University) where her dad, Joseph Lancaster Budd, was head of the Horticulture Department.

Helping other African Americans was important to George. He figured that if he studied botany (the science of plants), he could help Black farmers. George felt torn between being an artist or a scientist. But heading to Iowa State seemed like the right thing to do.

Winterset, Iowa, later became famous as the place where movie actor John Wayne was born. The Red Delicious apple was also first discovered nearby.

Not only did Etta Budd teach George painting, she also suggested he switch to studying science at Iowa State College and helped him find work to pay for his education.

At first Etta wondered how talented George was as a painter. She soon discovered that painting "was natural for him."

George was one of very few male students in Simpson College's fine arts department. While at the school, he also played basketball and performed on various instruments at concerts.

Agriculture grad

Since George wanted to learn about agriculture, Iowa State College was a great school for him. It was one of the first colleges in the country to focus on farming research.

Not everyone welcomed George when he arrived at the school in 1891. He was the first African American to attend the college, and some students insulted him because of their racial prejudice against Black people. George wasn't allowed to sleep in the dormitory. At first, he couldn't eat in the dining hall either — he had to eat in the basement with the kitchen staff. That changed after George's White friend Sophia Liston, from Simpson College days, spent a day with him.

Eventually George made a lot of friends at Iowa State, thanks to his cheerful personality. He joined many clubs — the debating club, German club, art club and the YMCA. As well, he started the campus agriculture society and ran prayer meetings. George was elected class poet and became the first trainer and masseur for the football team.

George also made time for painting. His friends encouraged him to exhibit his work at a state art show. George hesitated because he didn't have the money for a proper suit to wear to the show or for transportation there. But his friends bought him new clothes and a train ticket. George's work was a great success — one of his paintings was picked to represent Iowa at the World's Fair in Chicago, Illinois, in 1893.

At school, George earned top marks. The professors were impressed with his interests and skills, especially his talent for grafting plants — joining parts from different plants to create a new plant.

In 1894 George graduated with a Bachelor of Agriculture degree. His professors encouraged him to stay at Iowa State and get a Master's degree. The college also put him in charge of its greenhouse. George soon became Iowa State's first African American teacher.

George was now the only African American in the United States with advanced training in scientific agriculture. Soon many colleges, including Iowa State, wanted George as a professor. But when he was offered a job at an Alabama college for Black students, he accepted.

When George received his Bachelor of Agriculture degree from Iowa State in 1894, he was about 30 years old. He earned his Master's degree in 1896.

When George left Iowa State in 1896, students and professors gave him this microscope to remind him how much they would miss him.

"There is no short cut to achievement. Life requires thorough preparation — veneer isn't worth anything." — George

Exhibiting a painting at the World's Fair in Chicago was a thrill for George, especially when his painting won honorable mention.

George became a captain in the National Guard Student Battalion — that's the highest student rank.

At college, George wrote a paper about his experiments in breeding different types of amaryllis flowers.

WORLD'S FAIR GRAND COLUMBIAN CARNIVAL THE WORLD UNITED CHICAGO

CHICAGO DAY Oct. 9th 1893. Anniversary of the Fire.

MONSTER CONGERT · GRAND GHORUS — MOST GORGEOUS DISPLAY of FIREWORKS · EVER SEEN in AMERICA.

George was a member of the Creamery Operators Class at Iowa State. These students worked in the college's dairy.

Here I am in the back row, second from the right.

An African American school

"… education is the key to unlock the golden door of freedom to our people."

— George

Some students at Tuskegee learned how to make bricks and nails.

Tuskegee Normal and Industrial Institute, where George would soon be on staff, was originally named the Normal School for Colored Teachers. ("Normal school" is another name for a teacher-training school.) It opened on July 4, 1881, in Tuskegee (Tus-KEY-ghee), Alabama. Later called Tuskegee Institute and then Tuskegee University, its goal was to help African Americans succeed in their careers.

The end of the 1800s was a very difficult time for African Americans, especially in the South. Many had been freed from slavery only about 30 years earlier. Racial prejudice and regulations still kept Black people down. Southern states had laws that kept Whites and Blacks apart by creating separate schools, restaurants, parks and more. The ones for Whites were nearly always better than those for Black people.

Poverty also held African Americans back. The first president at Tuskegee, Booker T. Washington, believed that African Americans would only be treated equally when they showed their economic importance. Education was absolutely necessary, Booker felt. Going to school and college would help Black people find good jobs and gain equality with Whites.

Booker T. Washington had been born a slave in 1856 in Virginia. He wasn't allowed to attend school except to carry the books of his master's daughters. When slaves were freed, nine-year-old Booker began attending school himself. Each day he got up early to put in a full day's work before heading off to class. Booker graduated from the Hampton Normal and Agricultural Institute in Hampton, Virginia, and then became a teacher there.

When Booker was asked to be president of Tuskegee Institute, he showed his skill at fundraising. He persuaded both southern and northern White people to give the school the money and support it needed. Booker's dream was to make Tuskegee a school that would train African Americans for many careers besides teaching. He added courses in carpentry, dressmaking, blacksmithing, cooking and more.

Another of Booker's dreams was to create an agricultural experiment station. In 1896 he invited George to come to Tuskegee as a professor of agriculture and director of the station.

George said yes. He agreed with Booker's ideas about helping African Americans through education. Since George was used to moving around, he thought he would stay at Tuskegee for only four or five years. Actually he ended up teaching there for the rest of his life.

Booker T., our president, is in the middle of the front row.

Here's a photo of all the teachers at Tuskegee around 1900. George (circled) was the only professor in the agriculture department with a degree from a White college.

Booker T. Washington's middle name was Taliaferro (TOLL-i-ver). He became one of the most powerful African American leaders in the United States.

Students put up most of the buildings at Tuskegee. This taught them construction skills and saved the institute money.

These Tuskegee students are studying history. There were only 30 students in the first class at the school. By 1915 there were 1500 students.

Classroom and field

"Since new developments are the products of a creative mind, we must therefore stimulate and encourage that type of mind in every way possible."

— George

I urged farmers to plant crops such as soybeans and peanuts (shown here) because they make the soil better.

Life at Tuskegee was a big adjustment for George. He'd never lived in the Deep South or among large numbers of African Americans. As well, George was used to doing research in laboratories with lots of equipment. At Tuskegee, he had almost no money to equip his lab.

George was more than just the director of the agricultural experiment station at the college. His other jobs included teaching, designing the agriculture building, maintaining the school's weather station, landscaping the campus, educating local farmers, being the vet for the school's animals and testing the county's drinking water.

Before George arrived at Tuskegee, agriculture was an unpopular subject. Students didn't want to be farmers because they saw how hard their parents worked on farms and how little money they made. Even worse, some professors assigned farm chores as punishment. When George began teaching in October 1896, he had just 13 students. But by the next May, that number had doubled.

To help farmers near the school, Booker T. Washington had started an annual Farmers' Conference. George changed its name to the Farmers' Institute, increased the yearly meetings to monthly and added cooking demonstrations. In 1898 the participants held their first agricultural fair at Tuskegee. This grew from a one-day gathering for a few hundred people to events that lasted several days and were attended by thousands.

George felt many African American farmers in the South were still slaves — to cotton. Cotton sucks more nutrients out of soil than most plants, so cotton crops became poorer each year. In addition, most Blacks rented their farms from White owners. The farmers had to pay the owners a share of their crop. That left the farmers little money, so they borrowed to pay expenses. This trapped the African American farmers in a cycle of poverty.

To help the farmers, George suggested they try crop rotation. Instead of always planting cotton or another crop in the same field every year, George explained, they should plant a variety of crops. This would keep the soil from wearing out. Soybeans and peanuts would actually improve the soil while giving farmers food for their families.

Fertilizers improved soil, George knew, but poor farmers couldn't afford expensive chemicals. He suggested they use manure and compost — decomposed grasses, leaves and other plant materials. George's advice soon began to pay off.

To equip his lab at Tuskegee, George used anything he could find, such as this rolling pin and grater.

George was Tuskegee's highest-paid professor when he arrived. He had an amazing talent for inspiring his students.

Here are the professors in Tuskegee's agriculture department. George is sitting in the front row.

It was easy to see how poor and dry the soil around Tuskegee was. George worked hard to find easy, cheap ways for farmers to improve it.

One of George's many jobs was running the school's experiment station. This was about 8 ha (20 acres) where George and his students experimented with growing crops.

Jesup Wagon

"Neither time nor expense will be spared to make our work of direct benefit to every farmer."

— George

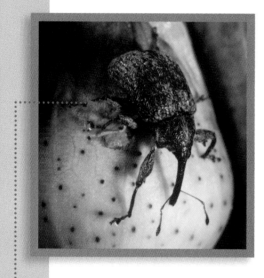

In the early 1900s, boll weevils devoured the bolls (the fluffy white parts) of the cotton plants but didn't touch peanut crops.

Booker and George continued to educate both students and farmers. But not all farmers could travel to Tuskegee, so George went to them. In 1904 Booker came up with the idea of a "school wagon" to take Tuskegee to the farmers. Funds came from Morris K. Jesup, a rich New Yorker, so the wagon was called the Jesup Agricultural Wagon.

George designed the first horse-drawn Jesup Wagon, and on May 24, 1906, his students took it on the road. For many years, the "movable school" was an example of Tuskegee's focus on the importance of education — for its students and for the community.

Farmers appreciated the seeds, plants and advice George gave them. He wanted them to switch from planting cotton to planting peanuts. George knew making such a big change was difficult, so he improved the cotton plants. His new cotton, Carver's Hybrid, produced a good crop and resisted damage from swarms of insects called boll weevils.

Students also appreciated George. After leaving Tuskegee, they often wrote to him and called him "Father" or "Dad Carver." George never had a family. He almost married in 1905, but the love affair ended. When asked why he never married, George replied, "I never had the time. Besides, what woman would want to live with a man who gets up at four o'clock in the morning — to talk to flowers?"

Some of the Tuskegee professors resented George. He was paid more than they were and had his own room — most bachelors shared. Also, it was hard to get to know George. He would rather work in his lab than go to parties.

George didn't always get along with Tuskegee's president either. Booker often criticized George for being disorganized. But the two men agreed about the importance of education for African Americans. When Booker died in 1915, George felt depressed for months.

Collecting money for a monument to Booker helped George recover. So did the new president, Robert Russa Moton, who asked him to help raise funds for Tuskegee. George was a popular speaker and raised a lot of money.

George soon became world famous because of his improvements to southern agriculture. In 1916 he was asked to join the advisory board of the National Agricultural Society. Later that year, George was elected a Fellow of the Royal Society of Arts of Great Britain.

George and his students used the Jesup Agricultural Wagon to visit farmers. They loaded it with seeds and plants, as well as helpful information.

Booker T. Washington was a practical organizer, while George was a creative dreamer. They often clashed, but when Booker died, George donated six months' salary to help build a monument in Booker's honor.

Not only did George teach his students about plants, he also reminded them of their manners, lent them money and ran Bible classes for them.

Here my students are learning about cows — from the inside out!

Peanut scientist

"When you can do the common things in life in an uncommon way, you will command the attention of the world."

— George

I once created a whole meal from peanuts — soup, vegetables, chicken, cookies, ice cream and coffee. Everything tasted delicious!

When George encouraged southern Black farmers to grow peanuts, they were already very familiar with the plant. It's one of the world's oldest crops. Many people still call peanuts "goobers" — the name comes from an African word, *n-guba*. Peanut plants are unusual because after their flowers bloom, a shoot sprouts from each flower's base. This "peg" burrows into the ground, where its tip swells into a peanut shell.

So many southern farmers followed George's suggestion to plant peanuts that soon the market was flooded. George felt that he'd created this problem, so he had to solve it. He locked himself in his lab and began inventing more uses for peanuts.

In the end, George created at least 325 peanut products — chili sauce, gasoline, shampoo, cream and fruit punch were just a few. (George didn't invent peanut butter — it had been created years earlier.) Sweet potatoes also inspired George. He made about 160 new products from them, including flour, ink, glue and vinegar.

Because of his products, the Department of Agriculture brought George to Washington, D.C., in 1918. World War I was causing food shortages, and officials hoped that George's flour substitute could help feed millions. But the war ended before this project was completed.

In 1920 George was the guest speaker for the United Peanut Association of America. To get to the meeting room, this well-known scientist had to take the freight elevator — the regular one was reserved for White people. Despite this example of racial prejudice, George dazzled the audience with his speech.

The Peanut Association decided that peanut farmers would be helped by a tariff, or tax, on peanuts from other countries. It would make American peanuts cheaper. George was chosen to speak in favor of the tariff before the U.S. House of Representatives, Committee on Ways and Means in January 1921. He was given only 10 minutes, but he so fascinated the congressmen that they let him talk as long as he wanted. Afterward, the Committee voted in favor of the tariff.

In 1928 George received the honor that meant most to him. Simpson College, his first college, awarded him an honorary Doctor of Science degree. George was proud to be recognized for the improvements he made to southern farming.

The famous inventor Thomas Edison wanted George to work in his lab. Some people say Edison offered George a huge salary of $200 000, but George chose to stay at Tuskegee.

During World War I, many farmers went overseas to fight and the United States ran short of food. So George's ideas for replacing meat and wheat got a lot of attention.

Some of the products George made from sweet potatoes included coconut, molasses, fabric dye, shoe polish and a type of rubber.

MEMBER OF
U.S. FOOD ADMINISTRATION

Food will win the war

We observe Meatless days
Wheatless days · Porkless days

and carry out all conservation rules
of the U.S. Food Administration.

George had a knack for interesting his audience in his research. Here he's demonstrating the wide range of peanut products he created.

Starting in 1898, George published many bulletins to help farmers grow good crops and improve worn-out soil.

BULLETIN NO. 31

JUNE 1925

How to Grow the Peanut and 105 Ways of Preparing it for Human Consumption

Edition
June 1936

By
GEORGE W. CARVER, M. S. in Agr.
Director

EXPERIMENTAL STATION
TUSKEGEE NORMAL AND INDUSTRIAL INSTITUTE
Tuskegee Institute, Alabama

Famous innovator

"Ninety-nine percent of the failures come from people who have the habit of making excuses."

— George

As the most famous Black scientist of his time, George continued to be a popular speaker with African American students. He also helped improve race relations by talking at White colleges. During the 1930s, George spoke at farmers' conferences, state fairs and meetings of the National Association for the Advancement of Colored People. He still faced racial prejudice but refused to be sidetracked by it — he preferred to work in his lab.

George kept on researching. In 1933 he discovered a surprising new benefit of peanut oil. Some women had complained that George's peanut oil lotion made their faces look fat. George thought perhaps the lotion made their skin expand as the oil's nutrients were absorbed. So he tried using peanut oil to massage a thin, weak boy. The child put on 14 kg (30 lbs.) in just a month!

Next George tried peanut oil massage on two patients with poliomyelitis (polio), a paralyzing disease. Soon one of the boys was able to walk again. Although one top doctor believed the peanut oil helped the boy, most doctors felt it was George's massage skills that did the trick. However, excitement about the new remedy led to a two-year peanut shortage!

In 1935 scientists became interested in a new subject called chemurgy. Today it's known as biochemical engineering — it focuses on finding industrial uses for farm products. George had been doing similar research for years, so now many people say he was the father of biochemical engineering.

George never got rich from his new products. He didn't think it was right to apply for patents (documents that give inventors legal rights to their inventions). George believed his discoveries were freely provided by God, so he felt it was wrong to make money from them. Other people pushed George to get patents, but he obtained only three: one for a cosmetic and two for paint products.

By 1938 George was more than 70 years old and had been at Tuskegee for 40 years. That year he became very ill with pernicious anemia. This blood disease is caused by the stomach's failure to absorb vitamin B_{12}. Doctors were afraid George might die. But they tried a new treatment and he was soon back in his lab.

In 1935 George identified the fungi that were destroying peanut crops. The U.S. Department of Agriculture honored him for this achievement.

President Franklin Delano Roosevelt was paralyzed with polio in 1921. George sent him peanut oil in 1933, and the president felt it helped his symptoms.

The Great Depression lasted from 1929 to 1939. Millions of Americans had no work and people were starving. George spoke out about the need to feed families cheaply.

Signs like this one from a bus station were common in George's time. They segregated White people from Black people.

COLORED WAITING ROOM

In 1938 the movie *The Story of Dr. Carver* was made. Two years later, George played himself in the movie *George Washington Carver*. Here's George in his lab at about this time.

In the 1940s, a small cosmetic company named Carvoline was formed. It made products such as this hair cream George created from peanuts.

CARVOLINE
Antiseptic
HAIR DRESSING
WITH PEANUT OIL AND LANOLIN
THE CARVOLINE CO. Birmingham, Ala

When I had time to relax, I still enjoyed knitting and painting.

Final research

*"I am not a finisher …
I am a blazer of trails.
Others must take up the
various trails of truth
and carry them on."*
— George

The famous carmaker Henry Ford (right) once said, "Professor Carver has taken Thomas Edison's place as the world's greatest living scientist."

After his illness, George didn't teach or work much in his lab. But he kept busy. In 1938 Tuskegee Institute decided to create the George Washington Carver Museum. George helped develop the plans, raise funds and organize the exhibits.

When the museum opened in 1939, thousands of people gathered to honor George. In the same year, George received the Roosevelt Medal for Outstanding Contribution to Southern Agriculture, as well as an honorary membership in the American Inventors Society.

George continued giving speeches in the early 1940s, but he had little energy. Still, at about age 77, he traveled to Dearborn, Michigan, for a very special occasion. Carmaker Henry Ford had created Greenfield Village, a collection of buildings important in American history. George joined Henry for the official opening of the George Washington Carver Cabin, a copy of George's childhood home in Diamond Grove.

George felt tired and weak when he returned to Tuskegee. Then in mid-December he suffered a painful fall. He died a few weeks later, on January 5, 1943. In his will, George donated all of his money to the George Washington Carver Foundation to help support agricultural research at Tuskegee.

Just a few months after he died, George's birthplace was made a national monument. It was only the third birthplace honored in this way and the first for an American who wasn't a president. Stamps and coins were created with George's picture on them. In the 1960s, both Simpson College and Iowa State University dedicated science buildings in his memory.

In 1969 George was elected to the Agricultural Hall of Fame in Kansas City, Kansas. He was also elected to the Hall of Fame for Great Americans in 1977, and to the National Inventors Hall of Fame in 1990. George would have appreciated these honors, because they drew attention to the achievements of African Americans.

Although George became world famous for creating hundreds of products from peanuts and sweet potatoes, his greatest achievement was the improvements he made to the lives of farmers in the South. Today George is remembered for his creativity and inventiveness, as well as his kindness, his love for his students and his generosity. George not only succeeded in his goal to help African Americans, but also continues to inspire people of all cultures around the world.

George is remembered for his focus on education for African Americans.

African American farmers continue to be inspired by George's innovations.

"It is not the style of clothes one wears ... nor the amount of money one has in the bank, that counts," said George. "It is simply service that measures success."

"A GREAT NAME CONTINUES IN THE SERVICE OF HUMANITY ——"

The USS *George Washington Carver* was named in honor of the famous inventor. It was one of the first U.S. Navy ships named for an African American.

The Tuskegee Airmen were America's first Black military airmen. They were trained at Tuskegee Institute during World War II (1939–1945).

George's life at a glance

1861–1865 The Civil War rages throughout the United States

1864 (about) George Carver is born in Diamond Grove, Missouri

George and his mother, Mary, are kidnapped by slave raiders. Moses Carver hires a neighbor to bring them back. George is returned, but Mary is never seen again.

1877 George leaves Diamond Grove for school in Neosho

1878 George lives in Fort Scott, Kansas, where he learns to cook and attends school

1879 March 27 — George flees Fort Scott when he sees an African American man lynched. He moves to Olathe and then Paola, both in Kansas.

1880–1884 George lives in Minneapolis, Kansas. He gives himself the middle initial "W," which comes to stand for "Washington."

1883 George returns to Missouri to see his brother Jim (who dies shortly afterward) and the Carvers

1884 George moves to Kansas City, Kansas, where he works as a typist in the telegraph office

1885 Highland College in Highland, Kansas, turns George down because he is an African American

1886–1889 George homesteads near the town of Beeler in Ness County, Kansas

1889 George moves to Winterset, Iowa, where he becomes a chef and runs a laundry business

1890 September 9 — George enrolls at Simpson College in Winterset, Iowa, to study piano and art

1891 George transfers to the Iowa State College of Agricultural and Mechanical Arts in Ames, Iowa

1893 One of George's paintings receives honorable mention at the World's Fair in Chicago, Illinois

1894 George earns a Bachelor of Agriculture Degree. He is the first African American graduate from Iowa State College.

George becomes a teacher at Iowa State

1896 George earns his Master of Agriculture Degree at Iowa State College

October 8 — George becomes a professor and Director of Agriculture at Tuskegee Normal and Industrial Institute (later Tuskegee University) in Tuskegee, Alabama

George increases Farmers' Institute meetings at Tuskegee from yearly to monthly

1898 The first Farmers' Institute agricultural fair is held at Tuskegee

George begins writing bulletins on various agricultural topics. The bulletins continue to be published for 45 years.

1903 George begins working with peanuts, the plant that will make him famous

1906 May 24 — The Jesup Wagon that George designed begins taking information out to farmers

1916 George joins the advisory board of the National Agricultural Society

George is elected a Fellow of the Royal Society of Arts of Great Britain

1918   George works with the Department of Agriculture in Washington, D.C., to fight food shortages caused by World War I (1914–1918)

1920   George is a guest speaker for the United Peanut Association of America

1921   George speaks to the U.S. House of Representatives, Committee on Ways and Means in support of a tariff (tax) on imported peanuts. The tariff is made law.

1923   George receives the Spingarn Medal from the National Association for the Advancement of Colored People (NAACP)

1928   George is awarded an honorary Doctor of Science degree from Simpson College

1933   George researches the use of peanut oil to treat polio

1935   George is appointed Collaborator, Mycology and Plant Disease Survey, with the Bureau of Plant Industry, U.S. Department of Agriculture

1937   June 2 — A bronze bust of George is unveiled at Tuskegee campus in honor of his 40 years at the college

1938   The film *The Story of Dr. Carver* is released

George becomes very ill with pernicious anemia, a disease that attacks red blood cells

1939   The George Washington Carver Museum at Tuskegee Institute is officially opened

George receives the Roosevelt Medal for Outstanding Contribution to Southern Agriculture

George is made an honorary member of the American Inventors Society

1940   George appears in the film *George Washington Carver*

1942   July — The George Washington Carver Cabin is opened at Greenfield Village in Dearborn, Michigan, by carmaker Henry Ford

1943   January 5 — George dies at Tuskegee Institute, several weeks after a bad fall

July 14 — U.S. Congress creates the George Washington Carver National Monument in Diamond, Missouri

The U.S. Navy cargo ship *George Washington Carver* is built

1947   A U.S. postage stamp is issued in honor of George

1951   A half-dollar coin is created with images of Booker T. Washington and George

1965   The submarine *George Washington Carver* is launched at Newport News, Virginia

Simpson College dedicates a science building in memory of George

1968   Iowa State University also dedicates a science building in George's honor

1969   George is elected to the Agricultural Hall of Fame in Kansas City, Kansas

1973   George is elected to the Hall of Fame for Great Americans

I never dreamed my boyhood love of plants would lead me to such an extraordinary life!

Visit George

George Washington Carver National Monument, Diamond, Missouri

Visit the place where George was born, and walk through the woods and fields that first inspired his love of nature.

George Washington Carver Museum, Tuskegee University, Tuskegee, Alabama

At this museum on the campus where George taught, you'll not only discover more about his research and lab work but also see his paintings and needlework.

George Washington Carver Museum, Austin, Texas

Find out about African American history at this museum. It has a special section for kids that's all about George and other African American scientists and inventors.

George Washington Carver Cabin, Greenfield Village, Dearborn, Michigan

Here you can see a copy of the cabin in Diamond, Missouri, where George was born, as well as other famous buildings in American history.

Tuskegee and Iowa State universities have great Web sites full of information about me and my work!

Index